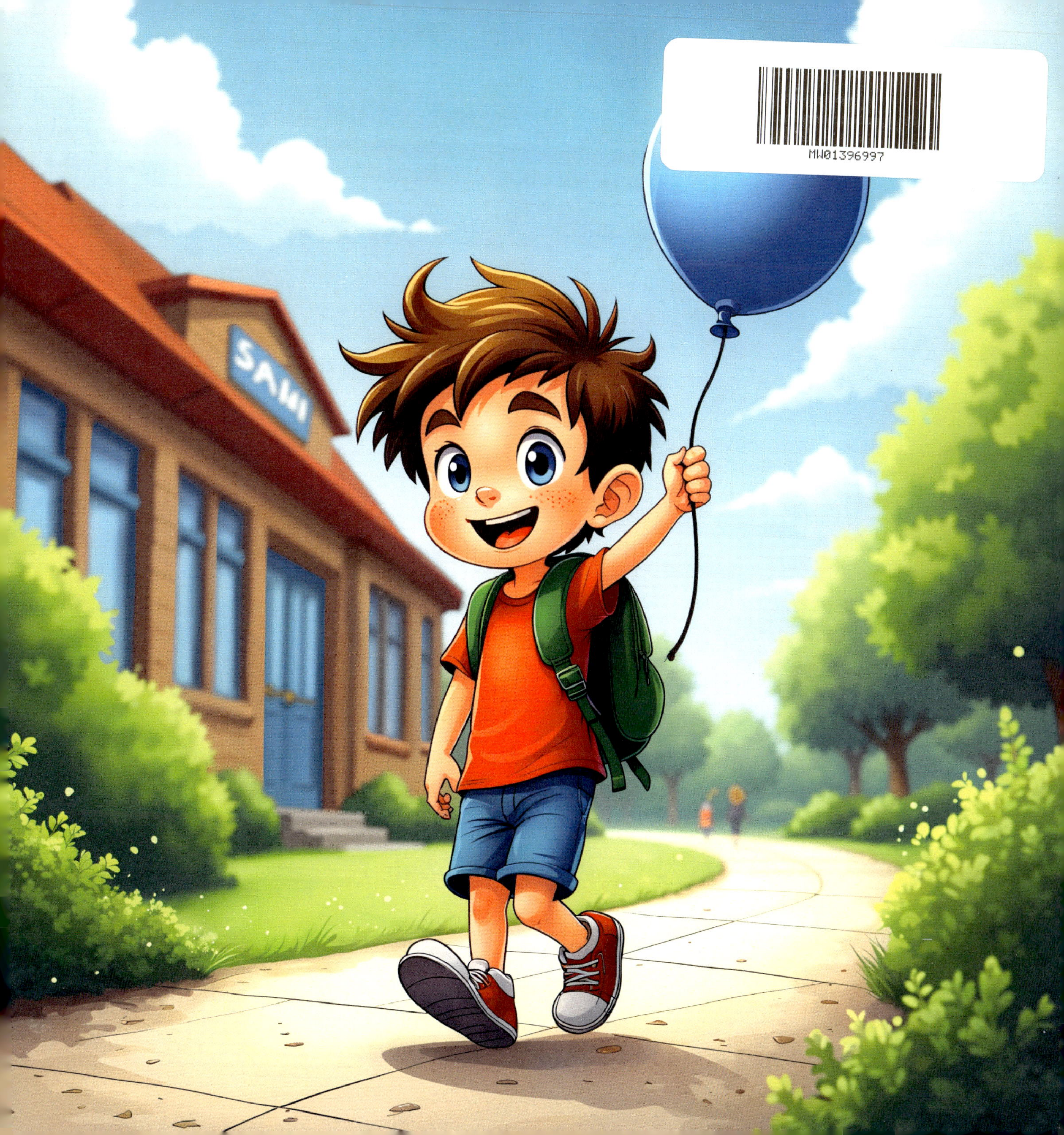

Coyright © 2025

All rights reserved. No part of this publication may be reproduced, distributed, or transmitted in any form or by any means, including photocopying, recording, or other electronic or mechanical methods, without the prior written permission of the publisher, except in the case of brief quotations embodied in critical reviews and certain other noncommercial uses permitted by copyright law.

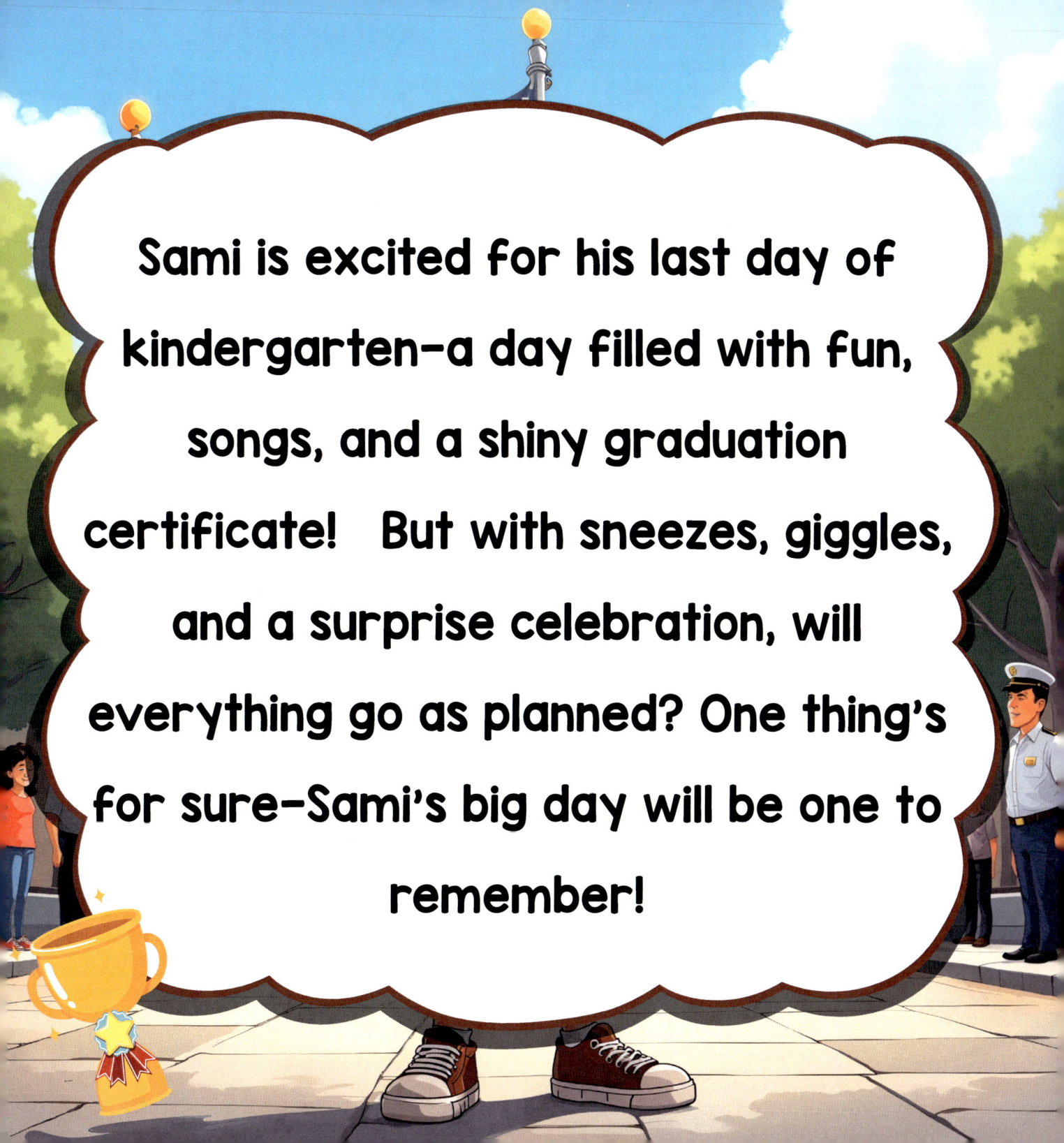

Sami is excited for his last day of kindergarten—a day filled with fun, songs, and a shiny graduation certificate! But with sneezes, giggles, and a surprise celebration, will everything go as planned? One thing's for sure—Sami's big day will be one to remember!

THE BIG DAY BEGINS

Sami, a curious 6-year-old boy, jumped out of bed with excitement. He wore his favorite red T-shirt, blue shorts, and brown sneakers. Today was the last day of kindergarten, and his school had a big graduation ceremony planned!

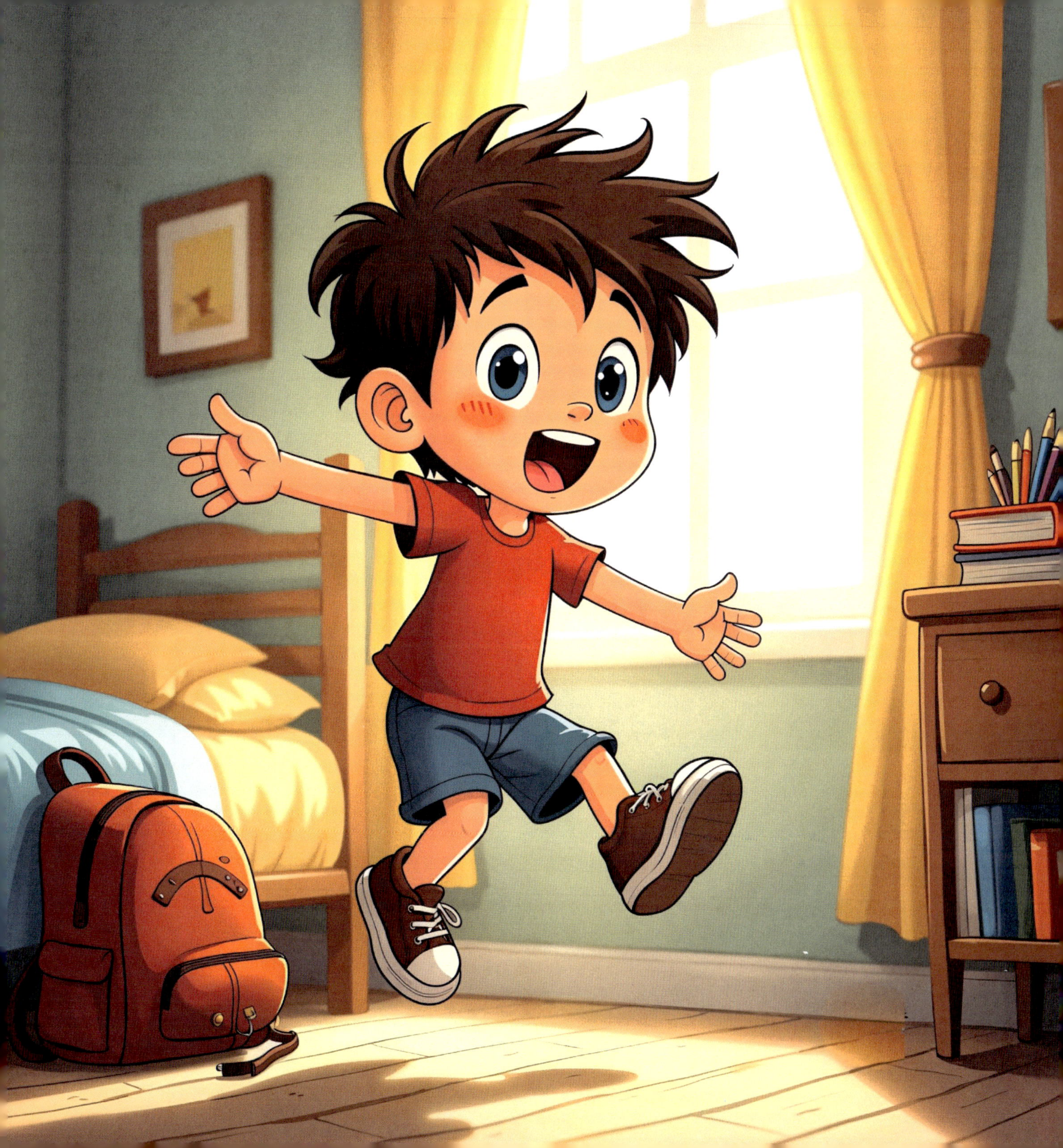

At breakfast, Sami could barely sit still. He stuffed a pancake into his mouth and wiggled in his chair. "I can't wait to sing on stage!" he cheered. His excitement bubbled over as he grabbed his backpack and dashed out the door. His heart thumped with anticipation-today was going to be special!

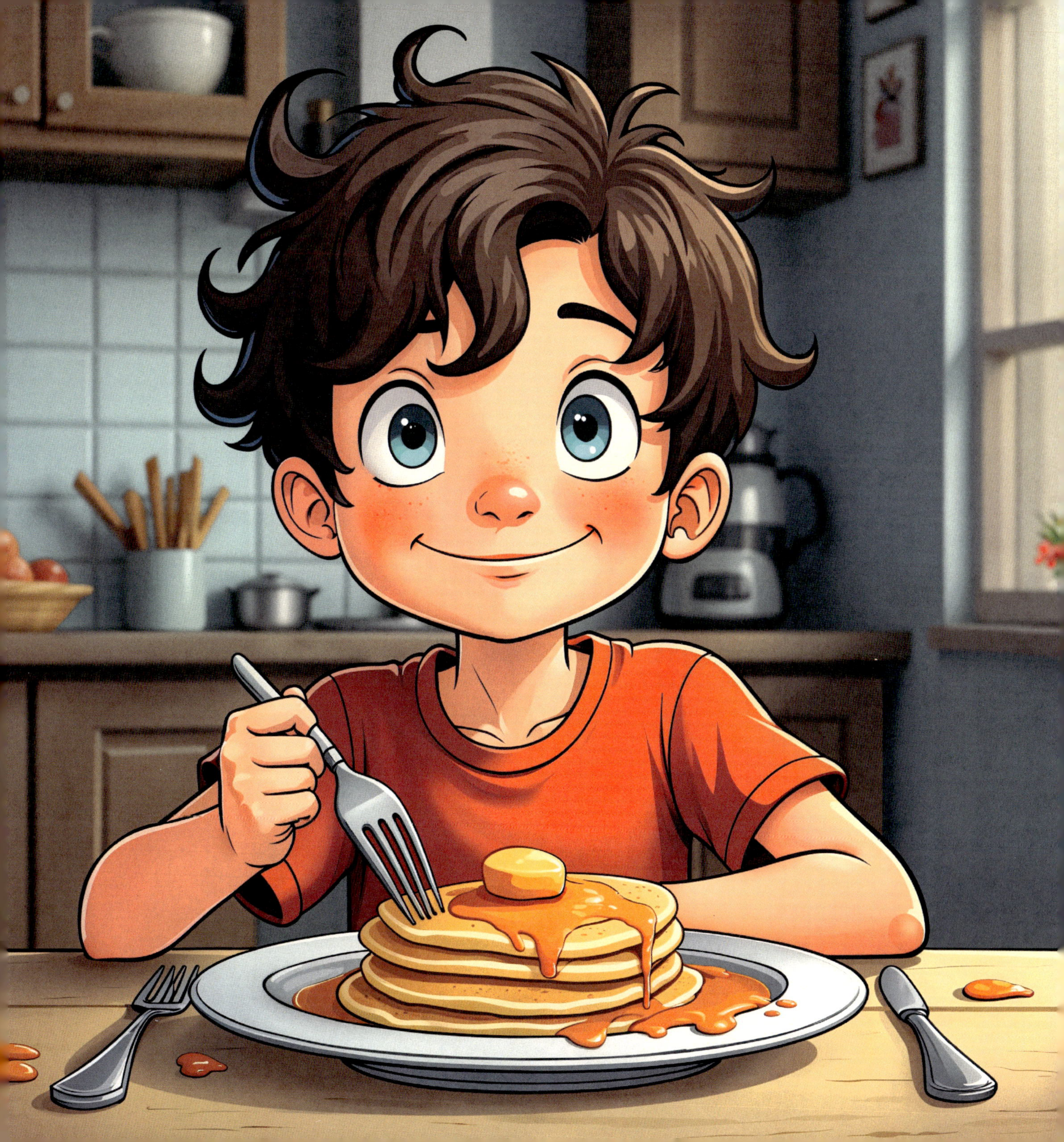

Sami raced to school, his sneakers slapping against the sidewalk. The school was decorated with balloons and a giant banner that read 'Congratulations, Kindergarten Graduates!'. His best friend Mia waved from the classroom door. 'Ready to be big kids?' she asked. Sami grinned. 'Ready as ever!'

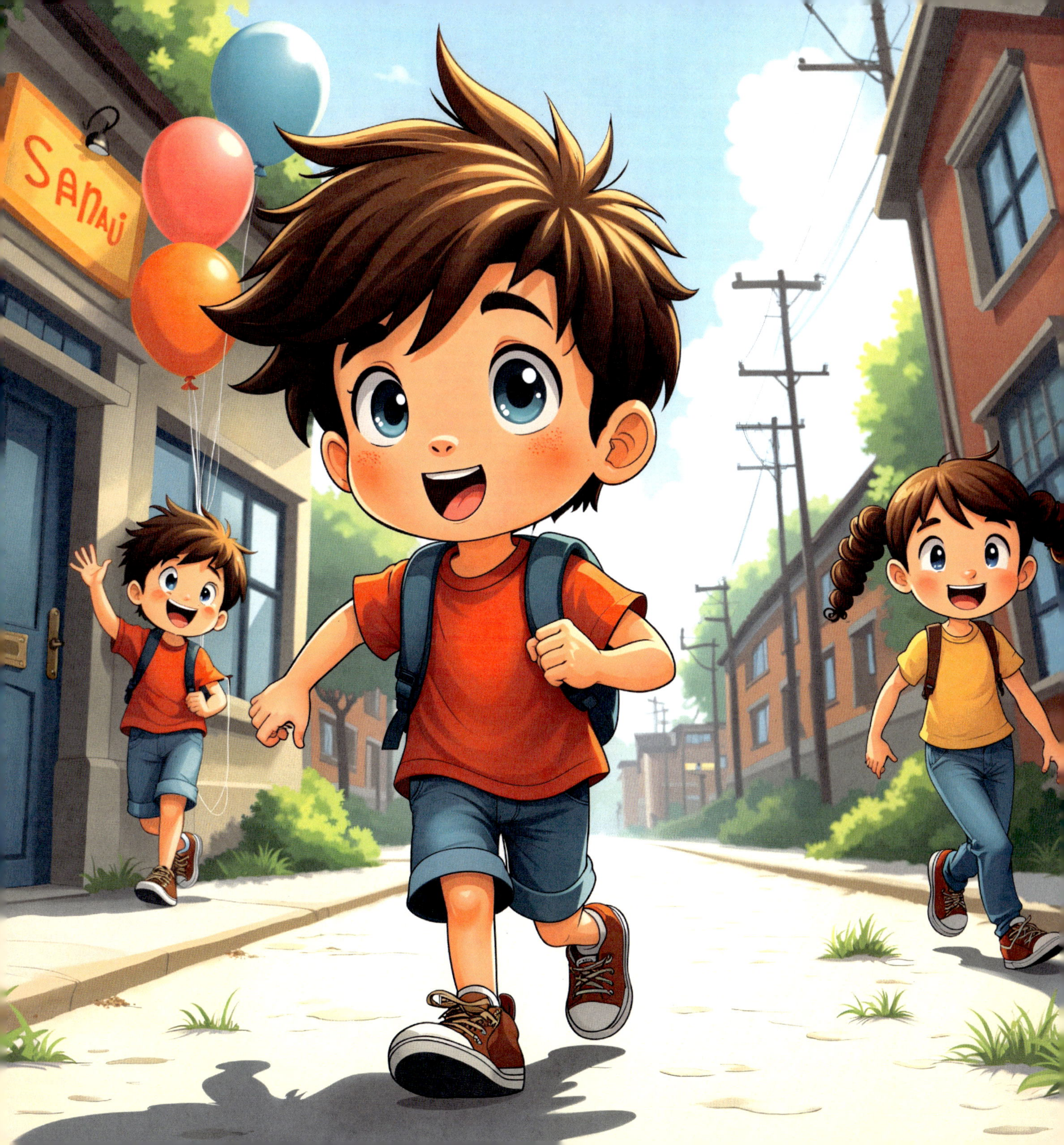
SANAU

THE REHEARSAL MISHAP

Inside the classroom, Sami and his friends lined up for rehearsal. Their teacher, Ms. Green, clapped her hands. 'Alright, everyone, let's practice the song!' Sami took a deep breath and–ACHOO! His sneeze sent his paper graduation cap flying across the room!

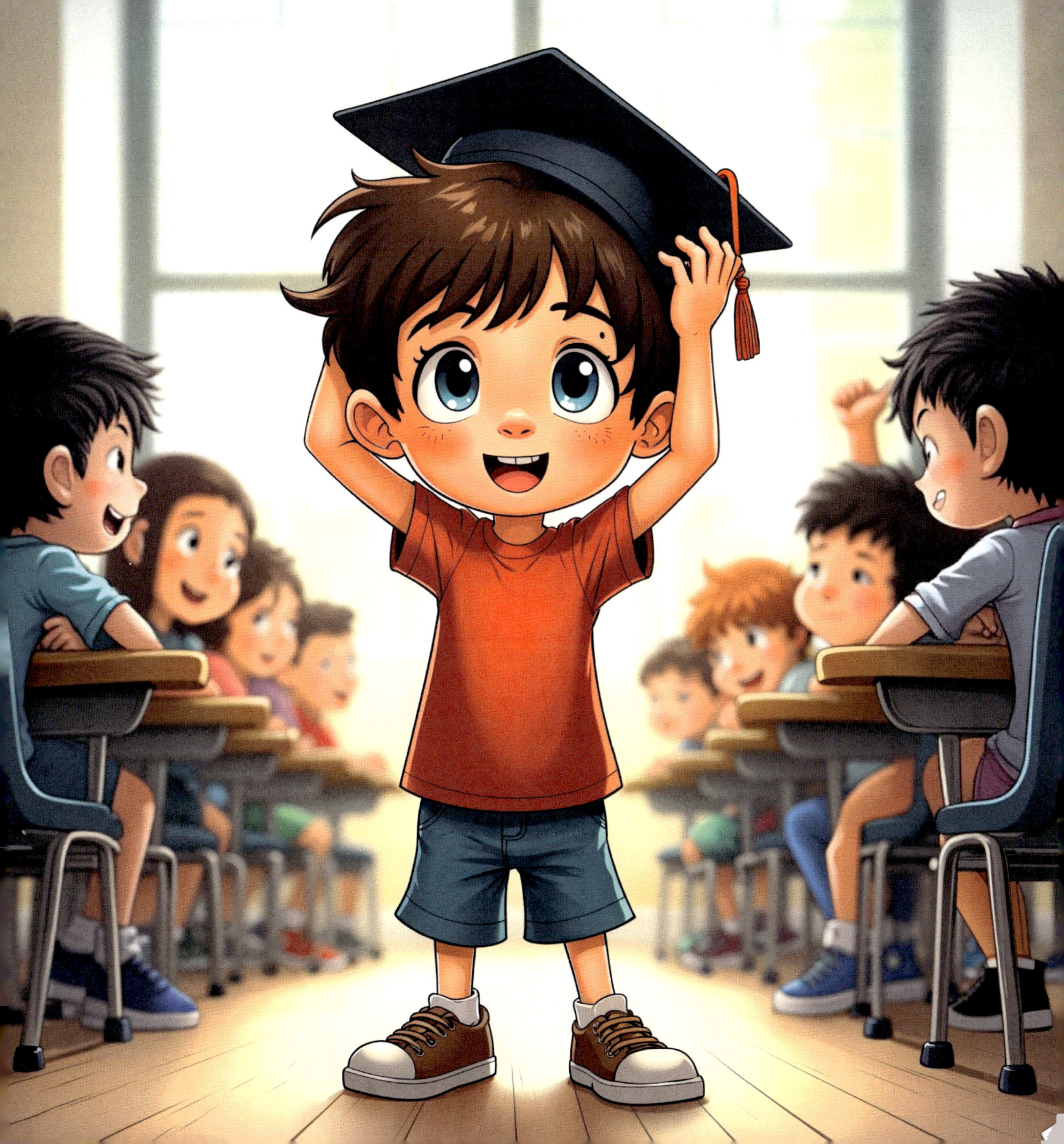

Mia giggled as she picked up Sami's cap. 'Maybe you should practice sneezing quieter!' she joked. Sami laughed, putting the cap back on. The class sang their song again, this time without sneezes—until someone's tummy rumbled! The whole room burst into laughter.

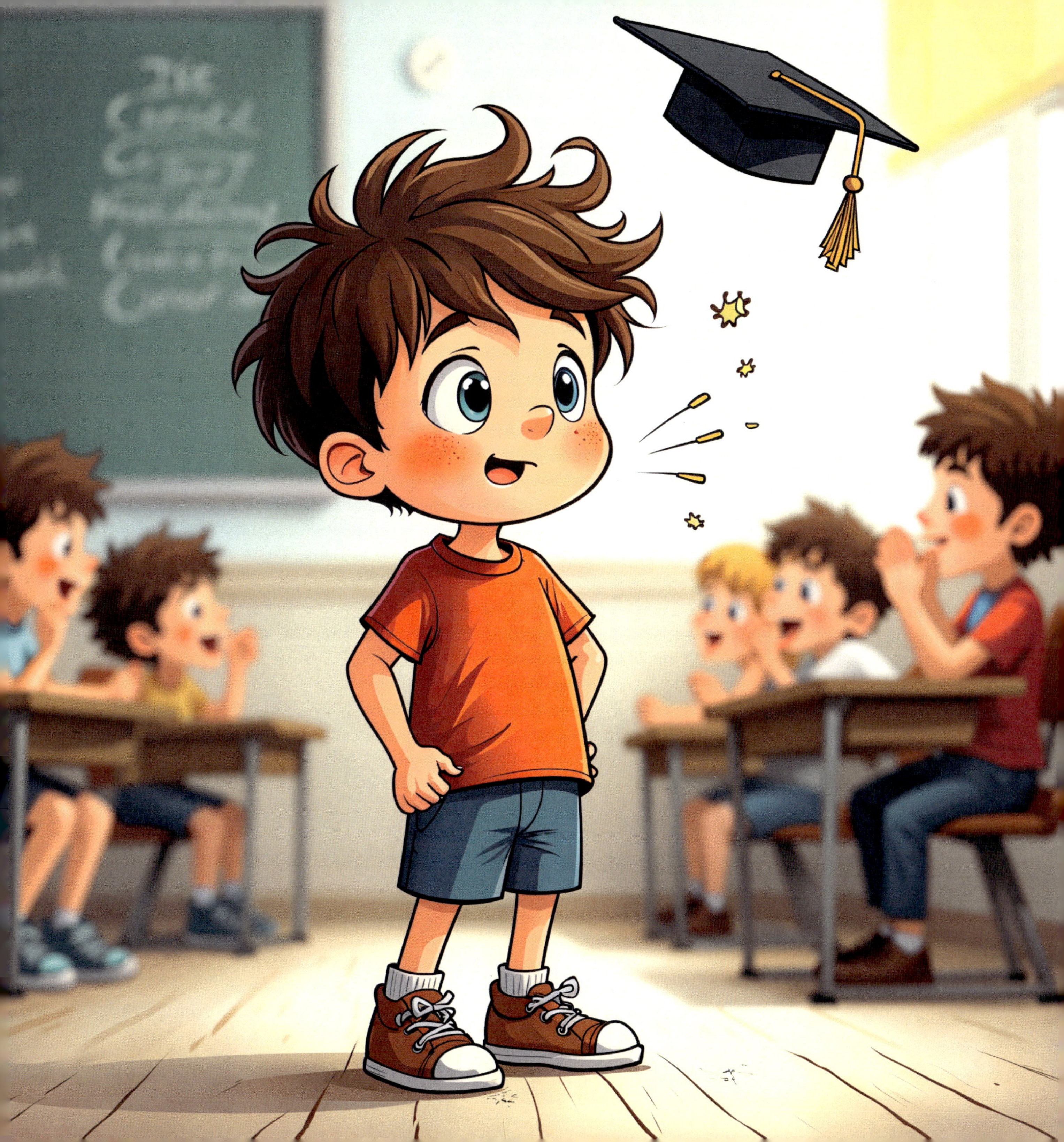

Ms. Green shook her head, smiling. 'Let's take a snack break before the real show.' Sami grabbed a juice box and took a big sip. 'This is the best last day ever!' he said. The class agreed, munching happily before their big moment on stage.

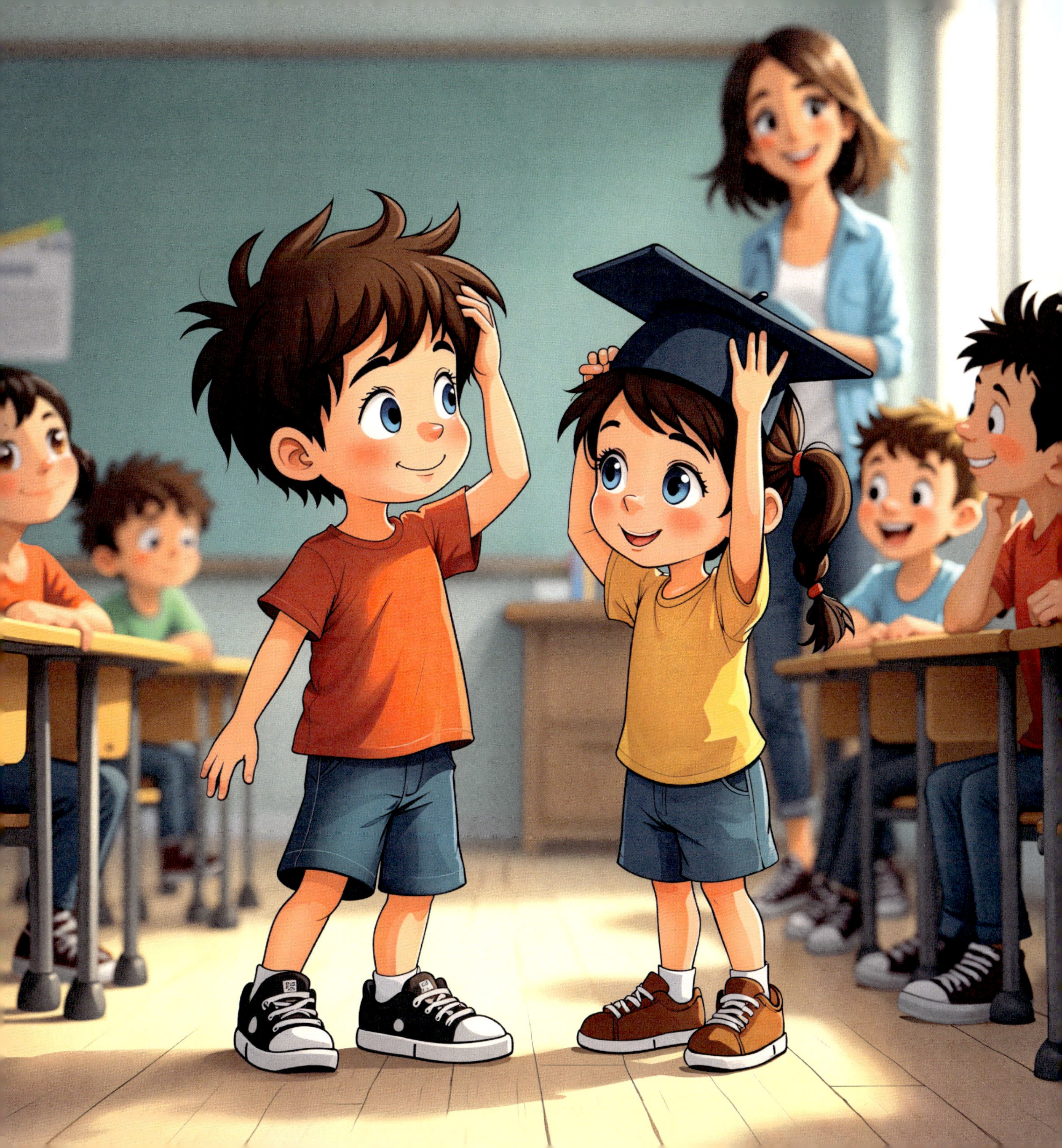

THE BIG GRADUATION SHOW

The gymnasium was packed with parents. Sami stood on stage, heart pounding, as the music started. He took a deep breath and began to sing with his classmates. His voice wobbled at first, but when he saw the smiling faces in the crowd, he gained confidence and sang louder.

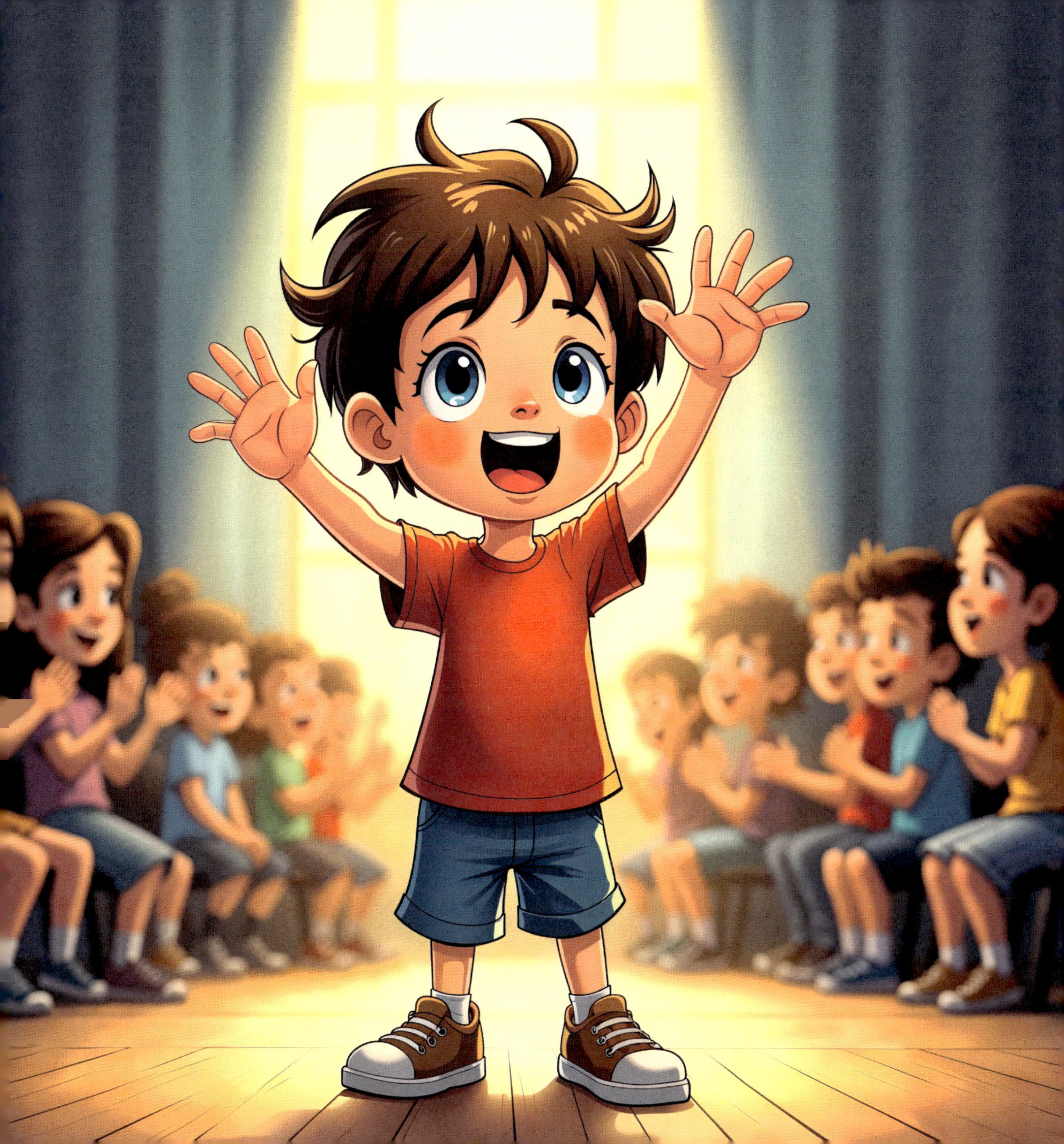

After the song, it was time for the certificates. Ms. Green called each student's name. 'Sami!' He walked up proudly and shook her hand. The audience cheered! 'Wow,' he whispered, staring at his shiny certificate. 'I really did it!'

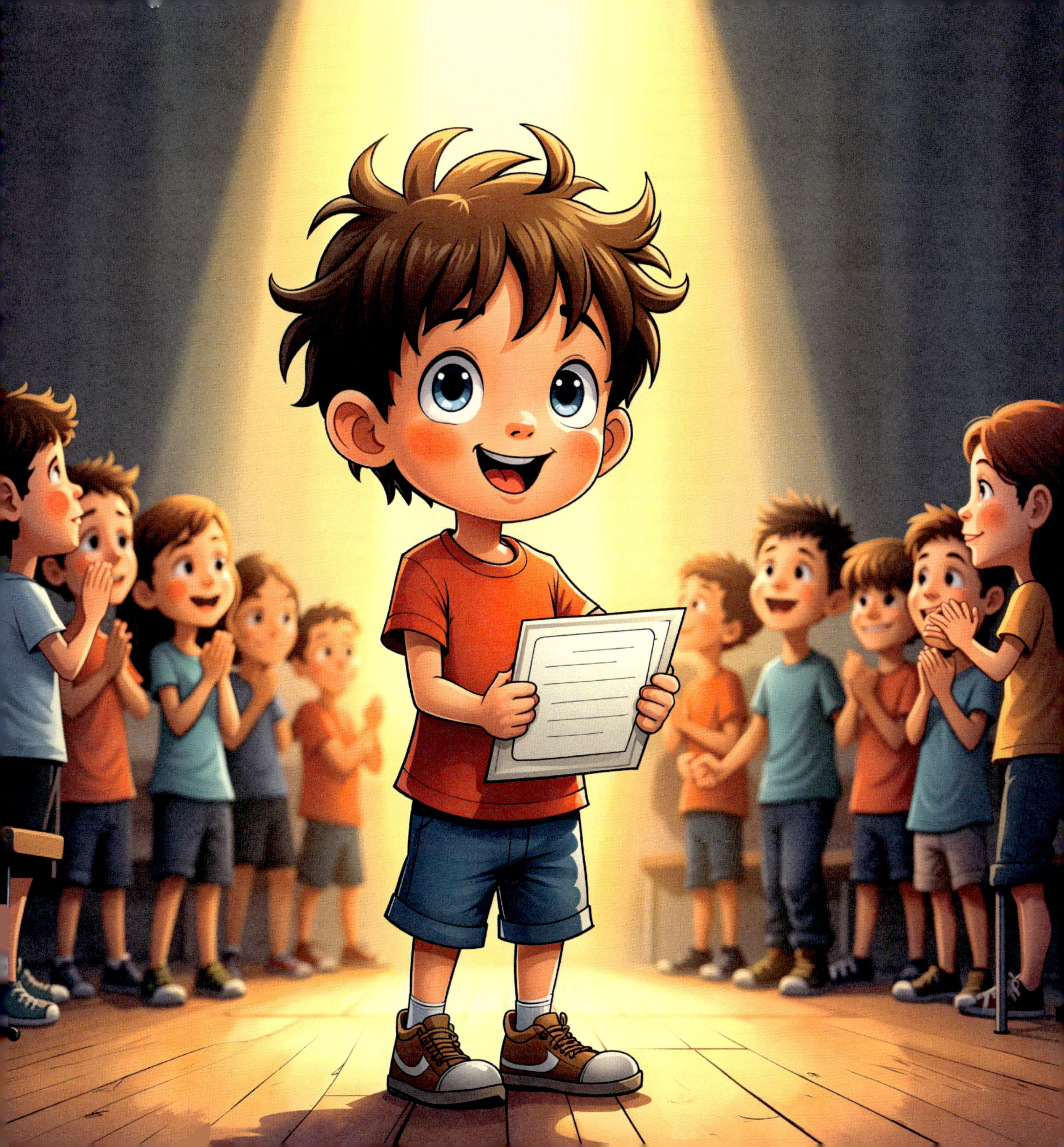

When the ceremony ended, Sami felt a rush of excitement. He had done it! He had finished kindergarten and was ready for first grade. But first, he had to celebrate-because a big moment like this deserved something extra special.

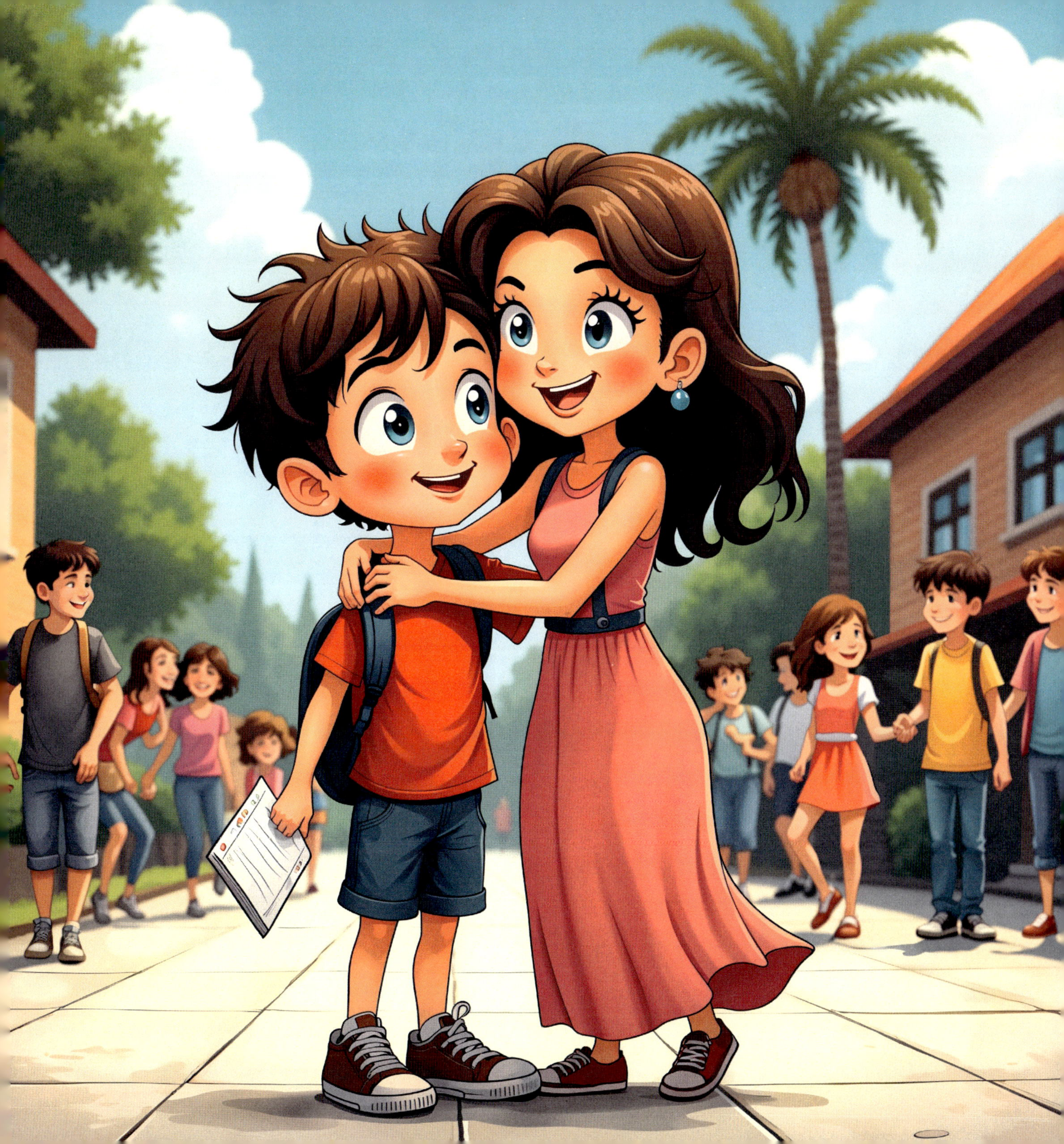

THE CELEBRATION BEGINS

After school, Sami skipped down the sidewalk, still holding his shiny graduation certificate. He had a big plan–celebrate with ice cream! He ran to the ice cream shop, eyes wide as he stared at all the colorful flavors. 'One giant chocolate sundae, please!' he said excitedly.

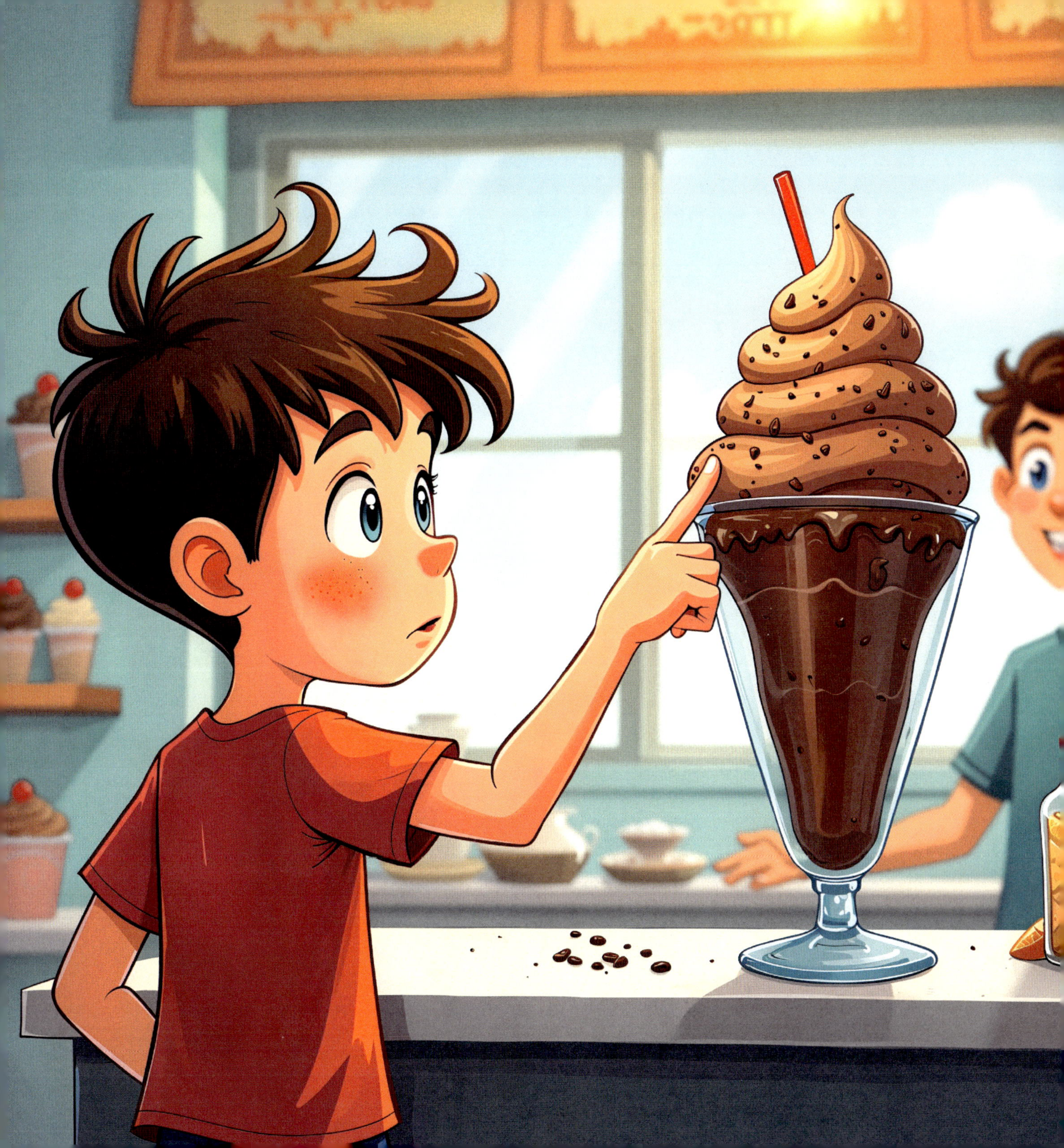

Sami found a seat near the window and dug into his sundae, the cold, chocolatey goodness making him smile. As he ate, he thought about all his kindergarten memories—finger painting, building the tallest block towers, and running races at recess. 'This was the best year ever!' he said between bites.

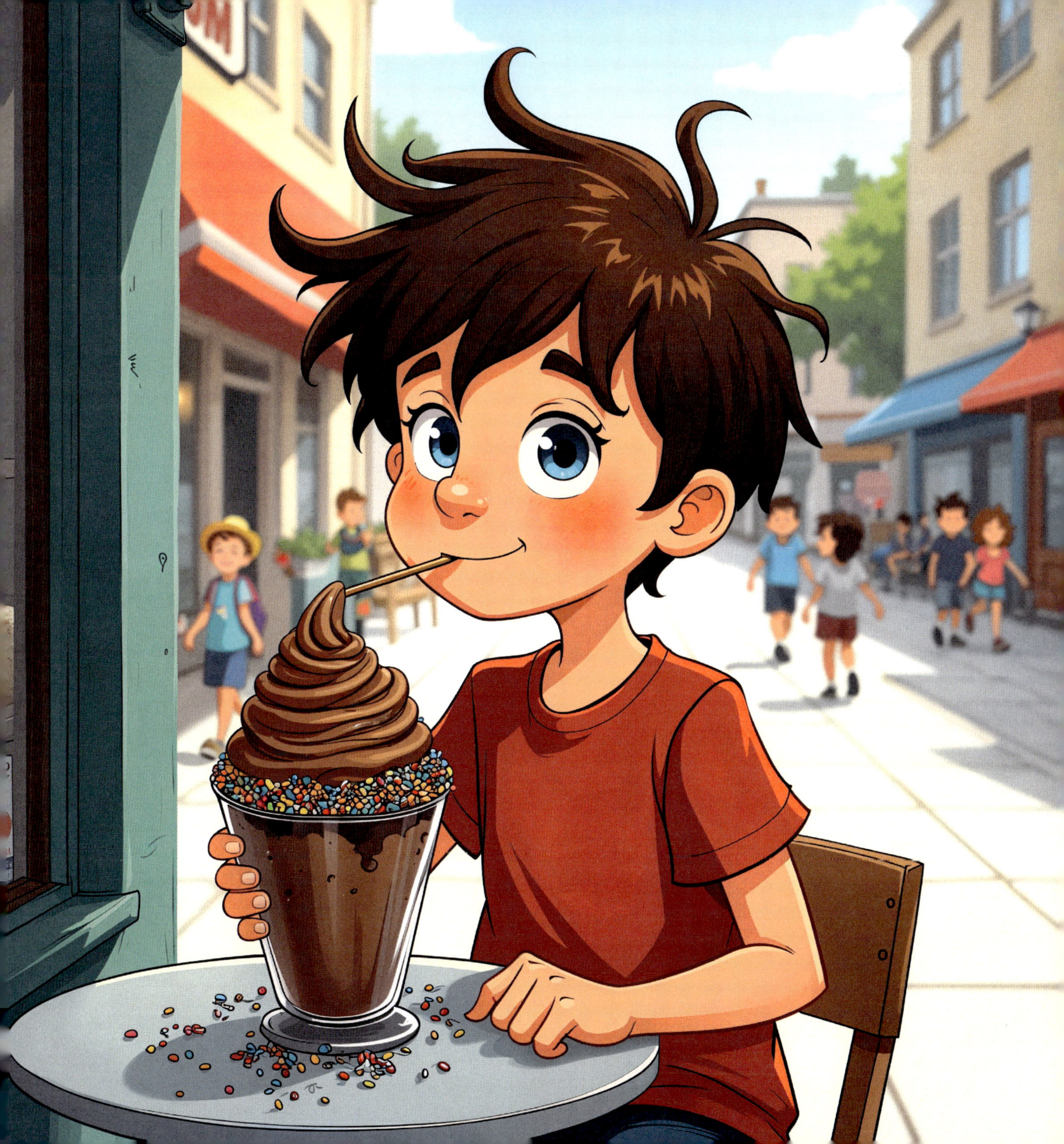

As he finished his ice cream, Sami held his graduation certificate proudly. 'I'm going to hang this on my wall!' he decided. The sun was setting as he walked home, feeling proud. First grade was just around the corner, but tonight was for celebrating-because he was officially a graduate!

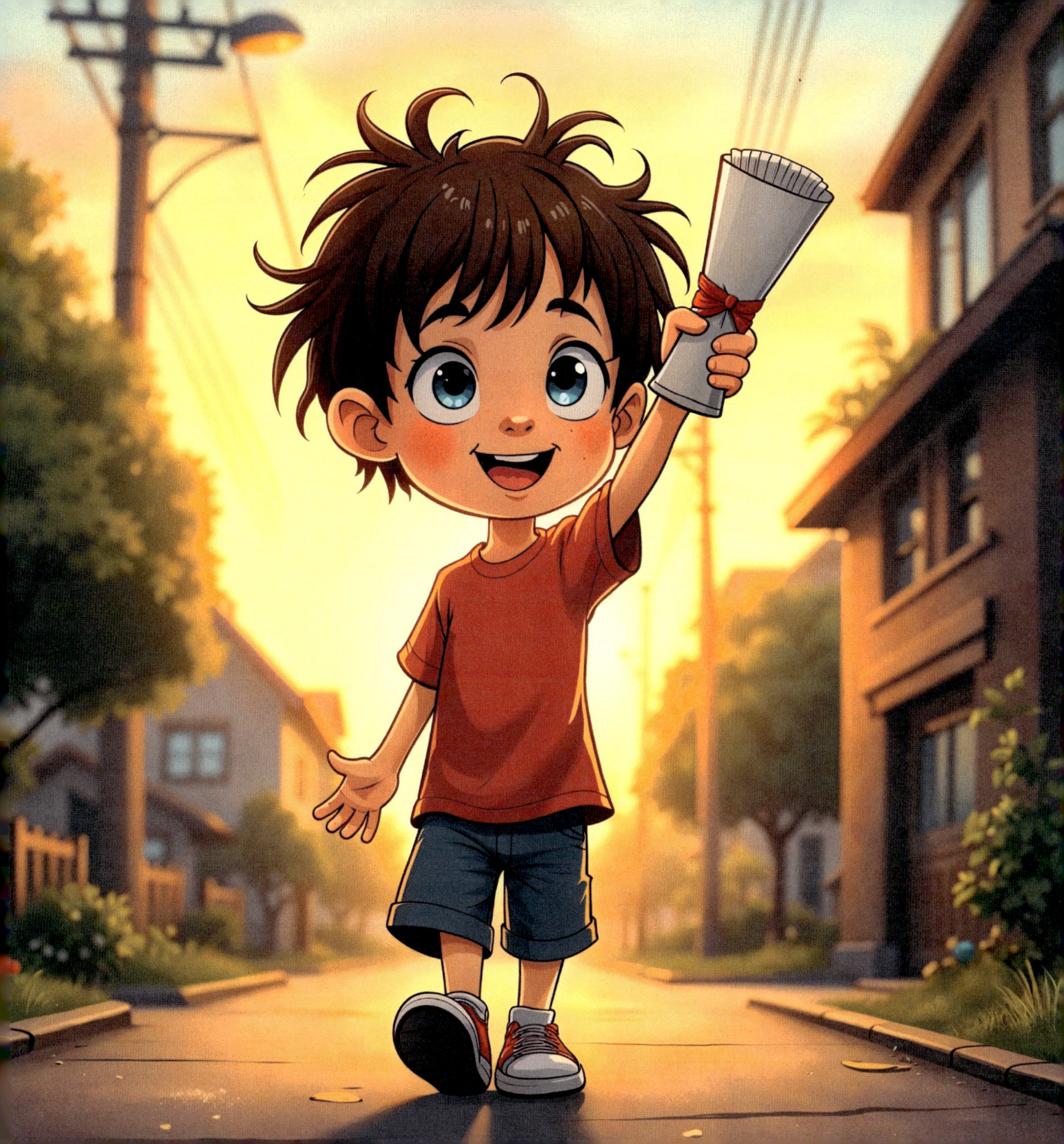

Circle the Correct Answer

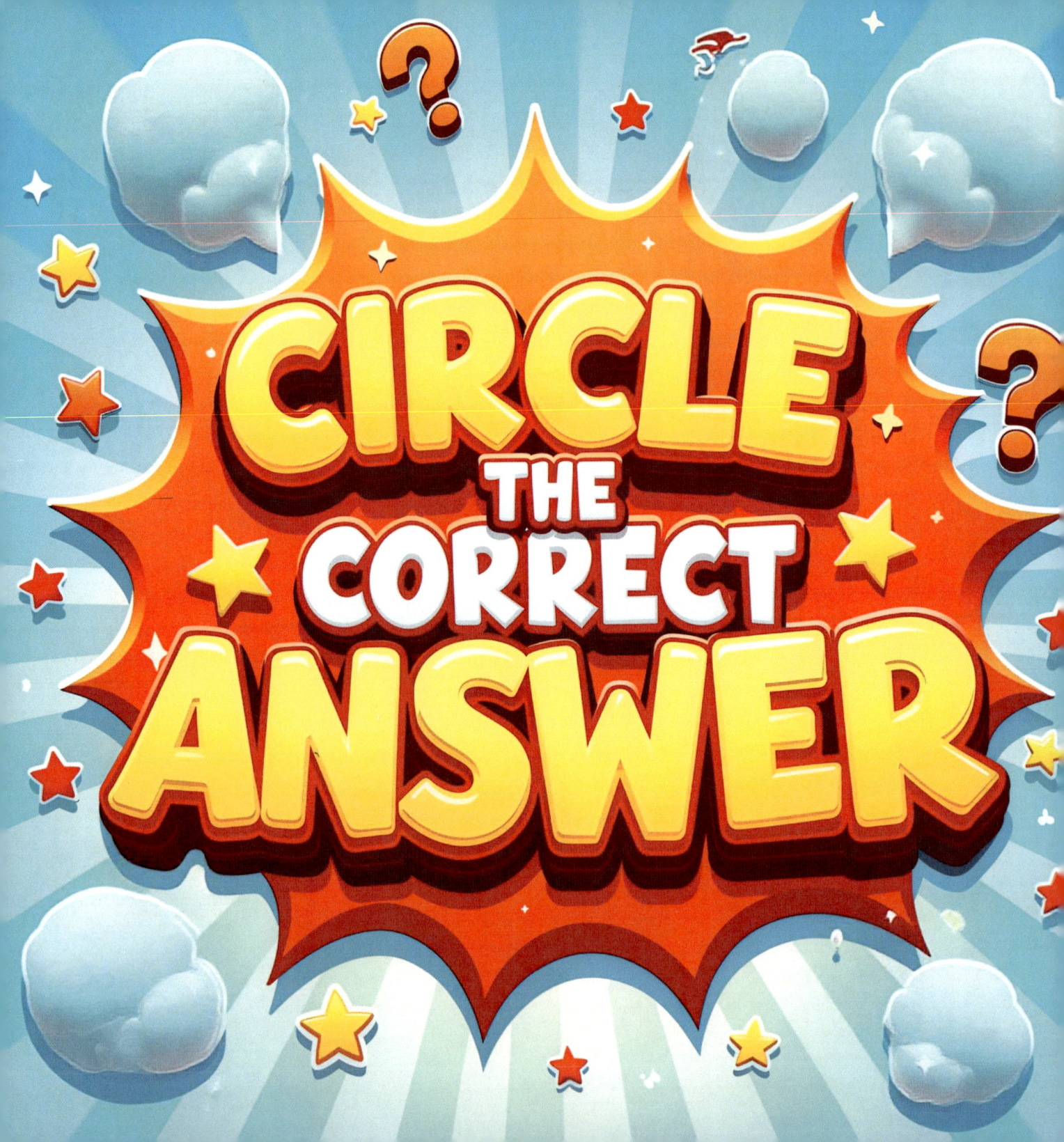

What did Sami wear?

A) Red T-shirt

B) Green sweater

C) Yellow jacket

Where did Sami go after school?

A) Ice cream shop

B) Toy store

C) Park playground

What flew off Sami's head?

A) Paper graduation cap

B) Magic hat

C) Birthday crown

What did Sami receive at graduation?

A) Certificate

B) Medal

C) Trophy

Made in the USA
Monee, IL
09 May 2025